HOW TO

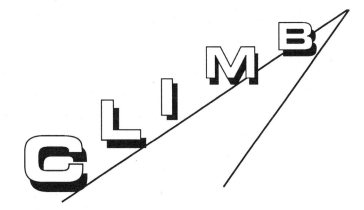

MT. WHITNEY

IN

ONE DAY

For Middle-Aged, Weekend
and Amateur Day Hikers

by
Sharon Baker-Salony

Cover Photo:	Winter morning over the Mount Whitney Crest *Photo courtesy of Robert Salony*
Back Cover:	Keeler Needle (foreground) and Crooks Peak (Formerly Day Needle) as seen from the 10-mile point at the base of Mount Whitney summit
Maps:	Aerial view of Mount Whitney's east face massif, Trail Crest, and John Muir Trail *Courtesy of Jim Stewart*
Photography:	All photography by the author unless otherwise indicated.

HOW TO CLIMB MOUNT WHITNEY IN ONE DAY

-First Edition-
Second Printing — April 1998
Third printing — August 2000

ISBN No. 0-9653073-0-I

Published by: Dublin-Shore Publications, Inc.
P.O. Box 818
Gardnerville, NV 89410-0818

Printed in the United States of America

DEDICATION

This book is dedicated to Jim and Bill Bees who taught me everything about survival hiking, whipped me into shape, and taught me how to keep going when I wanted to quit; my mother, Wilma Baker, and sister, Patricia Baker, who continued to believe in me after all these years; my husband, Bob, who allowed me to run away to spend the night alone on the mountain with a lot of strangers. . .

. . .And finally, Hulda Crooks, whose accomplishments on Mount Whitney have inspired hikers of all ages. Happy 100th birthday, Ms. Crooks, May 19,1996!

★ To see color photos of the Mount Whitney Trail or to order books, go to:
   www.mtwhitneyoneday.com

★ For more information on the ever-changing permit system and the Mount Whitney Trail, see:
   www.sierrawilderness.com

ACKNOWLEDGMENTS

Since no book is written alone, I would like to thank the following for making this endeavor possible:

Paul Hellweg for his excellent book *Mount Whitney Guide for Hikers and Climbers* and his valuable perusal of this manuscript;

Steve Reneker, who used Mount Whitney as a training ground to climb the Biggest One, Mount Everest, in relating his knowledge in the area of safety and helpful tips;

Jeff Galloway
Gary Suttles
The National Weather Service
The U.S. Forestry Service
REI Recreational Equipment
Dr. R. F. Sun of Semantech, for formatting, copyediting, typesetting, and guidance in the publishing process;
                                    and
Dr. Laura Schlessinger of KFI Talk Radio, whose philosophy of courage and perseverance helped me overcome the fears and doubts of writing this book.

Lastly — and most importantly — all the dozens of dear Mt. Whitney hikers whose names I will never know, and who sped me on to success by lending support, valuable hints and information by sharing with me their own "war stories" along the trail.

Any further helpful information concerning this climb is welcome, as are requests for assistance if you are having problems climbing Mt. Whitney.

"For it is the ultimate wisdom of the mountains that a man is never more a man than when he is striving for what is beyond his grasp, and that there is no conquest worth winning save that over his own weakness and fear."

..........*James Ramsey Ullman*
Author and mountaineer

"Life shrinks or expands in proportion to one's courage."

..........*Anais Nin*
Author

FORWARD

A couple of decades ago I didn't even know Mount Whitney existed. Even though I had driven past this mountain many times, I had to marvel at its unique cathedral-like structure which set it apart from all the other peaks in the Sierra Nevada. It wasn't until a colleague at work told me about this mountain and its claim to fame that I was bitten; not only was it beautiful and famous, but it was a challenge. I knew someday I *had* to climb it.

So, armed with a permit and absolutely no knowledge or experience, I set out on what I thought was an easy walk to the summit. Of course, I failed miserably. . . several times. . . beaten back by the elements and my own ignorance.

One humid but clear August day I dragged my sister and a few friends on a one-day excursion to Lone Pine Lake. All of us dressed in summer clothing and walked blithely up the trail — not knowing that a huge storm had gathered behind the Whitney Crest. Without much warning, it was down upon us in minutes — freezing, gale-force winds, rain, hail, lightning. And to top off everything we'd done wrong so far, all of us, soaked to the skin, took refuge in a rock cave at the edge of the lake to escape the lightning.

We immediately lapsed into the first stages of hypothermia, unable to flee to a lower elevation until the lightning had passed. My sister was sinking faster than the rest of us, and if not for the warmth she got by hugging her Labrador dog, Moose, she might not be with us here today.

I wouldn't say mountains can speak (although mountain lovers would agree they speak to your soul when you stand in their midst), but Whitney spoke to us that day.

Against all odds, we were lucky. The great mountain had decided to spare our little group of unprepared neophytes. Many souls, not so lucky, will walk the trail for eternity. That experience was my Baptism. From that day on, I learned to respect the ferocity of the Sierra mountain peaks; to read their moods and the skies; to choose the days when they were asleep and stay away on the days they raged. After numerous attempts, I was beaten physically and mentally. For many years I totally gave up all hope of ever climbing Whitney.

I have been there, done it, seen it and if I haven't seen it have been told about it. Stories of hikers in shorts and tank tops, caught at the summit in a freezing storm, with nothing other than toilet tissue with which to wrap their bare extremities, racing for their lives to get to a lower, warmer elevation; hikers so overcome by altitude sickness on Trail Crest they collapse, able to neither go up nor come down; hikers who packed so little food provisions they'd eaten it all by the time they'd gotten to Mirror Lake.

Just because Mount Whitney is so popular and so many people climb it, does not mean it's a "theme park ride" with risks and dangers surgically removed for the benefit of the masses.

On a quiet day the weather on the Whitney Trail is the most perfect you'll find on earth; on a bad day, it will kill you. Simple as that.

To climb Mount Whitney in one day is to accomplish the "marathon of hikes" and leave you feeling both exhausted and elated. Anyone with conditioning can climb it in 2 or 3 days. To climb it in one day takes that special "something" extra.

"Because it's there" is what Mount Whitney climbers will tell you when asked why they took on such a dangerous and taxing endeavor. Yet that is only part of the whole answer. The whole answer involves not in taking on the mountain, but as James Ramsey Ullman said, defeating our own fears and weaknesses. Triumphing over the mountain as it attempts to defeat you makes the victory all that more meaningful. In the end, the outside of a mountain is good for the inside of a person.

But the ultimate reward of finally standing on the summit is worth the risks that come with the package. Having fought freezing winds that all but throw you off the slopes, defeated distance and head-splitting altitude, and pushed your body farther and harder than you ever imagined leaves you with an experience and satisfaction you will never forget.

Every failed attempt I made for the summit was one more valuable lesson to get me to the top. I had read all the books concerning Whitney. While every one of them offer excellent hiking information, none catered to the amateur, older, or weekend hikers who all have special needs. And none detailed the arduous parts of the trail that would defeat hikers so close to their goal. Those issues will be documented in detail in this book.

Other than the excellent backpacking instruction I got from my son-in-law, Jim Bees, and his brother Bill, I picked up extra tips on the trail itself, having asked dozens of successful and seasoned hikers how they made the summit. I compiled all the information on these pages so that others could share my joy in having been to the top.

Climbing Mount Whitney will be fifty percent physical and fifty percent mental. The mountain will intimidate you if you let it. Do not give up! I am not an athlete by any means. I am of slight build and am not tall, but I made my first summit at age 49½. . . in one day! It was worth every tough, delicious minute.

Good hiking, and I'll see you at the summit!

TABLE OF CONTENTS

*"Mount Whitney from Portal
Labor Day Snow Storm."*

Mt. Whitney

1

INTRODUCTION

When you read the title of this book, your initial reaction was probably the same as most everyone who hears it — "You can do that?" Not only can Mount Whitney be climbed in a day, it's not even remotely out of the question. Difficult. . . yes — and not for everyone — but in no way impossible.

This book is for both those unfamiliar with the magnificent Sierra Nevada and Mount Whitney, and for the experienced who, for many reasons, have failed to make a successful climb but wish to someday stand on the summit.

To address beginners, Mount Whitney 14, 496', is the highest mountain in the <u>contiguous</u> United States, and one of the most popular and sought-after summits in the world. The highest mountain in the U.S. is Mt. McKinley (or *Denali*) in Alaska. At 20,320 feet, Mount McKinley is a treacherous mountain plagued by avalanches and Mt. Everest-like blizzard conditions, whose summit is extremely time-consuming to reach (A record fast climb to the summit is around 5 days!) and far beyond the means of most, not only physically, but financially.

That leaves Mount Whitney as a next-best major peak. Sitting high and distant enough to create a challenge, it's close enough to be within reach of hikers of all ages who thoroughly prepare to climb it. This makes Mount Whitney one of the few major peaks in the world whose summit can be reached in one day, instead of days, weeks and months, on a shoestring budget and with average conditioning. To scale Mount Whitney thus represents a near perfect "backyard adventure."

You will also be in the presence of a celebrity with an exciting past for Mount Whitney has also been a "movie star" for decades. Mt. Whitney and the surrounding peaks have doubled for the Himalayas in the classic film "Gunga Din," Mt. McKinley in the John Wayne movie "North to Alaska," the Andes in another John Wayne movie, "The Tycoon," the Colorado Rockies in countless westerns, and most recently the Mel Gibson movie "Maverick." Now almost every automobile commercial is shot in and around Whitney and the Alabama Hills (the huge, smooth brown rocks at the base of the Sierra range) as well as dozens of other commercials selling everything from brakes to running shoes. It's not unusual to see a film crew parked along Whitney Portal Road in the Alabama Hills any day of the week.

Luann   By Greg Evans

In the past twenty years, however, this peak has become so overwhelmingly popular that it is now the target of hikers and climbers from all over the world and is in danger of being "loved to death." On any summer day it is common to see day hikers from all over the United States as well as Europe and Asia. Less than fifty years ago, only a handful of hikers signed the book at the summit for the entire year. Now it's not unusual to see several *hundred* in line to sign the book on a single weekend afternoon! For this reason, beginning during the season of 1996, only 150 day hike permits will be allowed on the trail beyond

Lone Pine Lake. Only 50 "overnight" permits per day are issued for those wishing to attempt the climb in 2 or more days. Sundays and weekdays are far less requested than Saturdays and holiday weekends. For more information on permits, contact the Mount Whitney Ranger District, (760) 876-6200, 8:00 A.M.—4:30 P.M., Monday through Friday. Address: P.O. Box 8, Lone Pine, CA 93545

The best way to climb Mount Whitney is, of course, the 2- or 3- day overnight trip. However, if you are left out because of permit availability, your only alternative is to keep trying for overnight permits year after year; or try a one-day climb in which quotas are slightly more lenient; also, first come, "no show" permits for day hiking are usually available at the Mount 'Whitney Ranger Station in Lone Pine. You must be there in person the day of your desired hike to obtain these at 8:00 A.M.

REASONS TO DO IT IN ONE DAY

1. Permits:
    The limited availability - Even if you are one of the lucky few who do get permits (day or overnight), injury, altitude sickness or one summer thunderstorm could force you off the mountain and leave you with no chance for the summit until the following year. Then you must once more play "permit lottery." And for the middle-aged, you'll be one year *older.*

2. You're a Thoroughbred, not a mule:
    You dislike hauling half your household (food, bedding, water, shelter, etc.) on your back for miles straight up. Why carry 45 - 65 pounds or more on your back to survive 2 to 4 days when you can make it on much less than 20 pounds total in one day?

3. It is estimated that in 1994 over 40,000 people were in and about the 3 square miles of trails and forest surrounding Mt. Whitney severely taxing the resources. The less time you are on the mountain, the less your impact upon it.

4. Murphy's Law:
It's an *El Niño* year. It's early summer and the trail should be free of snow. It's taken you years to get an overnight permit. You've just traveled half way across the U.S. and on the day your hard-won permit is valid, Mother Nature dumps another foot of snow on the 15 feet of base, obliterating the trail beyond Lone Pine Lake. . . and the summit is socked in by *fog!*

The Mount Whitney Massif (Mount Whitney is center rear) with the Alabama Hills (remnants of an ancient mountain range) in foreground.

This guide is designed for those among us who are not superb athletes, but for the average weekend day hiker. For some (exempting childbirth, boot camp, and the Boston marathon), it will be the most grueling physical experience of a *lifetime*. For others, it will be merely the proverbial walk in the park. Climbing Mount Whitney is not for the faint of heart or slackers. This is a tough under-taking. Even professional climbers who have climbed exotic peaks dwarfing Mt. Whitney will testify that it's a surprisingly "tough little mountain." There is no easy way to do it, but this book will detail the easiest way to do the difficult. The reward of finally standing on the summit is worth it.

The following information contained in this book suggests a WORST CASE SCENARIO: meaning the difficulties the oldest, youngest, and nonathletic will encounter. Those in superb condition and/or whose ages fall in between these brackets may be able to ignore some of the physical problems to be described later.

CHAPTER I
PREPARATIONS &
CONDITIONING

**DO NOT ATTEMPT OR EXPECT TO CLIMB THIS
MOUNTAIN IF YOU HAVE SPENT THE LAST YEAR
SITTING AT A DESK.
YOU MUST MAKE PHYSICAL PREPARATIONS.**

The limited availability of permits has been covered. With
the growing U.S. population and the interest in Mount
Whitney, permits are going to become more difficult to
obtain and the demands may become so high that your
chances for successfully obtaining them for yourself on
the date(s) you desire will resemble odds in the state
lottery. So, if you do obtain permits, you're going to want
to make sure that you have a successful trip with the one
chance you have.

**READING THIS BOOK IS NO GUARANTEE OF A
SUCCESSFUL CLIMB, BUT ONLY HELPFUL ADVICE.
SUCCESS IS PURSUANT UPON THE PHYSICAL
CONDITIONING AND PREPARATION OF THE READER.**

This book is written for those with some hiking knowledge
and experience. If you are an absolute beginner, a recommended first book on preparing for Mt. Whitney would be
the *Mount Whitney Guide for Hikers and Climbers* by Paul
Hellweg and Scott McDonald, Canyon Publishing Com-
pany, 8561 Eatough Avenue, Canoga Park, CA 91304,
$7.^{95} or available at the Lone Pine Visitor Center, the

Whitney Ranger Station, the Whitney Portal Store and local gift shops.

Barring any major health problems (chronic heart problems, chronic lung problems, previous stroke, uncontrolled high blood pressure, Sickle Cell disease, or severe knee problems) anyone with proper conditioning and acclimatization (from an athletic teenager to the middle-aged and beyond) should be able to climb Mt. Whitney in a day.

People of all ages have conquered Mt. Whitney so it's not out of reach. You who are reading this guide are a hiker falling into the category somewhere between the legendary Hulda Crooks, who began climbing Mt. Whitney at age 66, and in the mid-1980s was making her 22nd summit at 88 years of age. (However, it took Ms. Crooks 4 days and an entourage of several assistants to accomplish her remarkable feat.) Or the 30-something Native American gentleman who, in 1994, ran nonstop from the portal to the summit in 2 hours and 15 minutes in mere possession of shoes, shorts and a flask of water. One-day round trips average between 12 and 15 hours; for the middle-aged, expect a nonstop 16- to 17-hour day.

Do not let the quick ascensions of fit hikers intimidate you as they "blow" you off the trail in their haste to reach the summit. Being too fit can defeat the day as there is the temptation to rush, thereby not letting the body adjust to the altitude. You might find these "rabbits" downed by severe altitude sickness at Trail Camp or the 97 switchbacks. The Mount Whitney trail has many ways of dealing with the overly confident.

Ascending the Mt. Whitney trail will put you through nearly 11 miles and ten-plus hours of relentless *up*. <u>Most</u>

who try will fail the first time. But one of the nice perks of doing a "One Day" is that permit availability is slightly more lenient and you might have the chance, in the case of permit cancellations, to come back the following days or weeks to try again.

Be sure not to drag along any friends, spouses, signifi-cant others or older children who are not totally desirous for the climb. If members of your party fail, as in the case of children, you may have to abandon your trip to accompany them back down to the Trailhead.

Ideally, your "One Day" will be a 2- to 3-day endeavor. The first day will be to acclimate yourself in Lone Pine using this day to drive the 13 miles west on the Whitney Portal Road out of Lone Pine to Whitney Portal. Take a 1- to 2-hour warm-up on the trail. You will not be going past Lone Pine Lake, so no permits, backpacks or supplies will be needed for this. This seems to "jump start" the physi-ological mechanisms of the body, waking it up to the demands of high altitude. Also, if you have never been on the Whitney trail, you can familiarize yourself in the day-light as you will be on this portion of the trail predawn and after dark.

To acclimate yourself, spend as much time as possible at Whitney Portal and try to camp overnight. However, if you can't sleep well in a vehicle and the thought of sleeping outside with the resident black bears is frightening, then by all means stay at a local motel. If you aren't fully rested the night before, you might not have a successful trip.

Also be sure the day before your ascent to eat a high-carbohydrate lunch at the portal or back down at a res-taurant in Lone Pine. Don't worry about your diet because you could lose up to 6 pounds on the daylong journey. In fact, **AVOID** dieting or any unnecessary stressing of the body for the week preceding your summit attempt as you will want your energy reserves full. These store in the liver and in body fat. This is the reason to carbo-load in the days before — to ensure that your body will have time to process its energy stores for the big day. If you have been laid out in bed the week preceding with a cold or flu, postpone the trip until your body heals and regains full strength.

The second day, make the summit, return down to Whitney Portal, then drive home or sleep over in Lone Pine. Make sure you reserve a room in advance; in the tourist season, all motels fill up early. Only drive home if it is close by (a four hour drive or less) and you are *positive* you can safely stay awake at the wheel. Spend at least one day resting as you will be <u>sore</u>.

So there you are. All one needs are good shoes, a pack full of water and food, warm clothes (see *Supplies*), a very early start and the mental determination to succeed. It shall be worth it!

CONDITIONING

Mt. Whitney, as grand and tempting as it is, intimidates hundreds of hikers each year into failing.

Therefore, the most important tools on this trip will be simple determination and a reasonably conditioned body. Without well thought-out and executed conditioning, your attempt to climb Mt. Whitney will not only be unsuccessful and possibly life-threatening, but it will be such a horrid experience it will leave you with absolutely no desire to

try again. Not only will it leave you in physical pain, but your psyche will also suffer the brunt of defeat which takes much longer to heal than sore muscles. . . if ever.

IF YOU ARE MIDDLE-AGED OR BEYOND
DO NOT **ATTEMPT THIS CLIMB WITHOUT SOME TYPE OF STRENUOUS DISTANCE AND ALTITUDE CONDITIONING!**

Walking 10.7 miles on the flat is not the same as 10.7 miles up into extreme altitude. That distance straight up from 8,360 feet to 14,496 feet can be as taxing and exhausting as many more miles on the flat. To illustrate how you'll feel, imagine strapping a heavy weight to your back and then walking up the stairs of the highest skyscraper in the world. . . *holding your breath!*

Therefore, you must precondition yourself with "climbing" miles to build those specific muscles you will need later. If you work in a high-rise, skip the elevator NOW and begin using the stairs. If you have access to a high school or college sports stadium, begin a program of running up and down the bleachers as frequently as possible. Stair-type exercise equipment is also good to keep you conditioned throughout the year along with bicycle riding which also builds stamina and muscle. Go on as many distance and hill climbing excursions as you can fit in your schedule. On mini-conditioning hikes, it's also a good idea to load your daypack with the weight you'll be carrying (camera and camcorders included), and at least a couple of times, so that your neck, shoulder and back muscles

will become accustomed to the weight and pulling.

Mount Whitney is graded a strenuous Class 1 (good footing and trail; no crampons or ice picks needed after the snow fields have melted in early summer). If you are lucky enough to live in or near the north and southwest, namely Southern California and Colorado, there are dozens of high elevation peaks. If you live in other parts of California or the nation, simply consult your state map. You will find the elevation of the highest mountain peaks closest to you. Then write or call the ranger station in that particular district. They will provide information on where to get trail maps. For the best source of highest summits in all of California, order the book *California County Summits* by Gary Suttle, Wilderness Press, 2440 Bancroft Way, Berkeley, CA 94704, (510) 843-8080, $14.⁹⁵. This book denotes altitudes, maps, mileages, time frames, and class rating of each hike. If there are absolutely no mountains of significant altitude where you live and you have some time, Horseshoe Meadows right "next door" to Mt. Whitney has a trailhead of 10,040 feet, and a 14.4-mile round trip hike will take you to New Army Pass at an elevation of 12,385 feet. (Horseshoe Meadow Road runs south off the Whitney Portal Road, 3½ miles west of Highway 395. It's a 20-mile drive to the road's end.) Again, contact the Mount Whitney Ranger District for more information. (For another high altitude hike, see Chapter III, Hazards, under Altitude Sickness.)

A good starting hike of the season will be a 5- to 10-mile round trip with as much altitude gain as you can manage. If you are 40 or over, the first hikes of the season will probably be miserable. Your heart will jackhammer, your breath will be in gasps, and your muscles will be so sore you'll barely be able to walk the next day. You might be tempted to give up at this point. **DON'T!** Each consecutive weekend that you go out and push yourself further than the week before will cause wonderful things to happen to your body. It will become progressively stronger and more efficient. The periods of soreness will shorten after each workout. Through the course of your conditioning hikes, if you spend several weeks at high altitudes, increased red blood corpuscle formation will make the delivery of oxygen to muscles more efficient. Another plus is that once you have subjected your body to the rigors of high altitude, some of your conditioning can remain with you to the following year, or allow you to "bounce" back into condition more quickly. However, if you are middle-aged or beyond and you are going to try for the Whitney summit, you *must* recondition with several strenuous hikes at the beginning of each hiking season.

In rarefied air, your body will only be able to perform at 60% of its ability. If you are a heavy smoker, either quit, cut down, or forget about any chances for ever standing atop Mt. Whitney. Oxygen is needed in airplanes flying above 12,000 feet. You are going far beyond this *ON YOUR OWN POWER!* Your lungs will need all the help you can give them.

Any women pregnant or who suspect they might be should also check with a physician before going.

Change your diet. Cut down on fats and cholesterol-laden foods. Your heart will also be working at full capacity. If you are concerned and have an existing heart condition or family history of heart-related problems, **CHECK WITH YOUR PHYSICIAN BEFORE PLACING YOURSELF IN JEOPARDY.**

The following information is a summary of <u>Resting</u> Pulse Rates and the degree of existing physical condition associated with each rate:

Below 50 Beats Per Minute (bpm) . . . . . Your state of physical fitness is excellent.

50-70 bpm . . . . .You are in a good state of fitness, but you can still improve with more exercise.

70-90 bpm . . . . Your state of fitness is average.

90-120 bpm . . . . .Your state of fitness is below average. See your physician on how much you should extend yourself.

Above 120 bpm . . . . . .You are in poor condition. Do not attempt any rigorous exercise before you consult a doctor.

One rule of thumb. To determine your *maximum* heartbeat, simply subtract your age from 220. The difference will be the heartbeats-per-minute rate you should not exceed. Example: 220 beats per minute minus 50 years of age equals 170 bpm.

If you are middle-aged and are concerned about your heart rate, you can check your pulse while you hike by using your fingertips (not the thumb as it also has a pulse and you may be counting beats twice). Place your fingertip in the indentation of your wrist below your thumb. Count your pulse beats either for 20 seconds and multiplying that figure by 3, or count for 15 seconds and then multiply that figure by 4 (e.g, 20 pulses in 15 seconds x 4 = 80bpm *or* 20 pulses in 20 seconds x 3 = 60bpm). If you're not good at calculating math in your head, just count each heartbeat for a minute. Even at rest on the highest parts of the Whitney trail, your heartbeats could hover around your maximum rate. If you have cleared yourself with your physician and are still concerned,

heart-rate monitors can be purchased at better sporting goods stores. Prices start at the low one-hundred dollars and up.

Jogging also will increase heart and lung capacities as well as stamina and muscle conditioning, but again, if you can find hills or steep grades on which to train, by all means this is better than on the flat. If you are interested in getting fit from a "couch potato" start, an excellent book is *Galloway's Book On Running* by Jeff Galloway which is available from Shelter Publications, Inc., P.O.Box 279, Bolinas, CA 94924, $12.⁰⁰. This excellent book helps you set up a running and exercise program, charts your progress, and gives in-depth descriptions of the physiological changes you can expect.

Prep hike goals of 14 to 17 miles <u>round trip</u> involving altitude are substantial training for the nearly 22-mile Whitney round trip. If you physically prepare wisely and thoroughly (meaning distance and altitude), you could find that by the time you reach Trail Camp at 6 miles up and 12,039 feet, you're feeling as if your body has just had a "warm-up." If you have achieved this point of advanced conditioning, your odds for a successful summit will probably be 100%.

"HITTING THE WALL" (as compiled from *Galloway's Book On Running:*

To simply explain the mechanics of this phenomenon, if you push yourself too far for too long, your body will protect itself by ultimately breaking down. Muscles are only capable of performing the amount of work they have been accustomed to doing during the previous 7 to 14 days.

If you've never pushed yourself past a 5-mile distance hike, don't expect your body to function well (or at all) on a 22-mile round trip.

This is a breakdown of what happens to cause you to "Hit the Wall."

Glycogen is the fuel made from carbohydrates (breads, fruits, starches and natural sugars). This is stored in the muscle cells with extra going to the liver. When the body has absorbed all the glycogen it can, all remaining glycogen is turned to fat and stored in the body as such. This is the body's most rapid and convenient energy source. Glycogen, however, produces waste products such as lactic acid which, if not washed out of the muscles by the bloodstream, causes muscles to become tight and sore with overuse.

At the beginning of your hike, initial stores of glycogen will rapidly deplete and the body will transition to using fat deposits as its fuel source. As long as the body is not being pushed far beyond that which it's been conditioned, fat-burning will be the primary source of energy. Fat is a "clean-burning fuel" but demands lots of oxygen for usage.

But as the distance and altitude wears on, an unconditioned body or one pushed past its conditioned distance will become overwhelmed. When muscles are pushed too far, they will demand even more oxygen than the body can supply, and in this situation will switch from burning fat to again burning your limited supply of glycogen. Rapidly-burning glycogen pours large amounts of lactic acid and wastes into the muscles faster than they can be removed. The muscles thus become tight and burn. You find yourself struggling, one miserable step at a time, and slowing down. This is when trouble begins because glycogen is the *ONLY* fuel used by the brain.

And when glycogen levels become critically low, survival defenses take over and reserve what's left for the brain. When the brain senses a low supply, it protects itself by making it difficult for you to concentrate on finishing the journey. . . or even rationalizing the *merest* excuse to QUIT.

This can occur even in hikers who are conditioned to go the distance. The chemical processes of your body and brain are recognizing the severe outlay of energy and are merely trying to self-preserve. If you are in proper condition and *know* you are not in a life-threatening state, you must mentally override this process if you are to complete the journey. Simply recognizing that this unique phenomenon can and *will* occur is the first step in overriding it. Accompanying trail maps (pages 73, 82 and 86) will pinpoint the approximate areas you might "Hit the Wall."

The only tried and true way to override your mind's rationalizations to quit is to simply point your feet in the direction of the summit and *keep* them going!

To avoid hitting the wall, rest for only 5 minutes at a time. In those first 5 minutes your muscles will regain approximately ⅓ of their lost energy. In the next 5 minutes, though, your muscles recharge only about 5% more, yet will begin to stiffen. The best strategy of all is to take in lots of carbohydrates and liquids, then set a steady, reasonable pace that allows your muscles to renew energy at the same rate they fatigue.

Some energy saving tips are:

1)   The "Lock Step" (or "Rest Step") —
     As each leg comes forward and the foot touches
     the ground, lock the knee of that leg. This gives
     enough pause for the other leg to rest before
     coming forward. Repeat as each foot touches the
     ground.

2)   Pacing —
     If you can carry on a steady conversation without
     becoming winded, you are moving at a nice, steady
     pace which covers more ground than quick bursts
     of speed, followed by long rest stops.

Remember: There is a fine line between recognizing the
difference of the mind's desire to quit and the body's
actual *necessity* to quit. For the sake of a permit or a
stubborn ego, <u>do not</u> push a body that is truly failing, or
force it through severe altitude sickness or anything that
is life-threatening.

CHAPTER II
SUPPLIES

As stated in the reasons to do a "One Day," you will have no need to haul bedding, shelter or large amounts of food, water and clothing. You must realize, of course, that even on a one-day trip, your *life* could depend on what supplies you include or omit. It's better to be overly prepared for what may never happen.

Pack wisely. If in a group, there's no need for everyone to carry lots of the same thing. Delegate supplies among you (e.g., one carries the camcorder, another the camera); stronger members carry some supplies of the weaker, older or smaller.

EQUIPMENT:

Backpacks: (see photo #1)
Other than good shoes, the backpack you select is your most important piece of equipment, for it will carry the necessary supplies to keep you comfortable and possibly *alive*.

The following is a compilation and description of the available backpacks available nowadays. Whatever your choice, keep in mind that for greatest comfort and chance of success, you must select a pack with adjustable shoulder straps and sternum strap (keeps shoulder straps from sliding off the shoulders). Most importantly, a *padded* hip belt is mandatory. Without a hip belt, all packs (when full) hang heavy on the neck and shoulders, supported *only* by those parts of the anatomy. By trip's end (or long before), the resulting pain could be excruciating as you're going to be pushing up against weight and possibly buffeting winds. Be aware that a thin, unpadded hip belt could wear blisters on your hip bones in the course of the day.

Example "A"

Selecting A Backpack

When purchasing a pack, one size *does not* fit all! A short-trunked person carrying a pack so long that it impedes leg movement will be as miserable as a bodybuilder type wearing a pack too narrow for his or her chest and shoulders. To be sure you select the right size pack for you, measure your back length by placing a tape measure on the bump of your neck and down your spine to where the small of your back joins the top of your hip bone.

Approximate back measurements are as follows:

Small —	16"–19"
Medium —	18"–21"
Large —	20"–23"

Select a reputable sporting goods chain with knowledge-able salespeople to help you find the backpack that fits. Since you will not be spending the night on the mountain, you won't need the expensive mobile-home-sized external frame backpacks *(Example "A", Page 20)* onto which tents, sleeping bags and cooking gear are lashed.

• <u>Frameless rucksacks</u> are OK; just make sure they have <u>padded</u>, adjustable shoulder straps and hip belt. A sternum strap is also necessary to keep shoulder straps from sliding off.

• <u>Internal frame</u> packs work best for day hiking. They are light, bend and move with the body contours, and do not have the metal frame which could attract lightning. Again, choose one with padded shoulder straps, sternum straps, and hip belts.

Whichever pack you choose, a minimum pack size of about 1,700 cubic inches and up should be large enough to accommodate enough gear for the day journey. Take into consideration that the bigger you are, the more you're going to eat and drink. However, watch the weights of backpacks. The more pockets, padding and accessories, the heavier the pack. Try not to exceed two-and-a-half pounds if you are a child or of slight stature because carrying the extra poundage for this distance and altitude will wear away valuable energy reserves. Depending on what you're carrying, decide between <u>canvas</u> and <u>nylon</u> packs. Canvas is thicker and, therefore, heavier in weight than nylon, but is also more durable and less apt to be

punctured or torn. However, canvas gets even heavier if it gets wet. If you're small or not really strong, but gentle on your equipment, nylon is definitely the way to go.

Top-Loading vs Panel-Loading

• Top-loading packs are like a tube that you stuff. They carry a lot, but if you pack something you need down at the bottom, or it works its way down, you'll have to dump everything out to reach it, then re-pack. *(See Photo #1, right)*

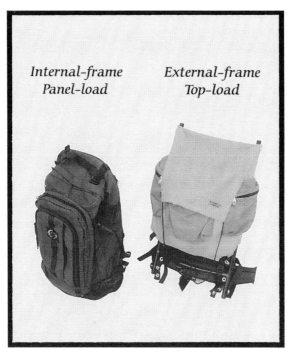

Internal-frame
Panel-load

External-frame
Top-load

Photo #1
Left: Panel-load canvas, interior frame backpack, 3½ lbs.
Right: Nylon top-load exterior frame backpack, 1½ lbs.

• Panel-loading packs *(See Photo #2)* have one to three piggybacked sections with inverted **U**-shaped zippers that open out like a mailbox. The largest section, which is closest to the body, is good for heavy, large supplies. Frequently accessed articles like food, energy bars and toilet tissue (and your wilderness entry permit) can be carried in the smaller, outermost sections. New and improved styles of backpacks even come with detachable lumbar packs, so that you drop your main pack at Trail Camp or Trail Crest and just carry a minimum to the summit.

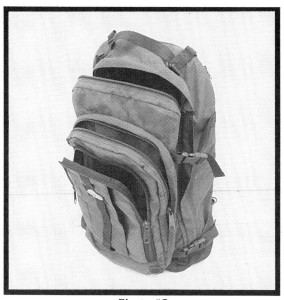

Photo #2
Close-up of panel-load internal frame pack.
Notice ease of finding essentials instead of digging
down to the bottom, such as with a top-load pack.

Again, when purchasing a backpack, select a reputable sporting goods chain with knowledgeable salespeople. Most of these chains have samples of various types of backpacks already loaded with supplies in the weight you'll be carrying. After you choose the pack you like, put it on and walk around for a while to see if the pack is ill-fitting at any point. If so, select another until you find the one that fits you *perfectly*. You will not regret doing this. It's worth the time and effort and could be the difference between a successful trip and failure.

One lucky note — Expensive isn't necessarily the best. Buy what fits!

Packing

Use creative packing. By folding and "rolling" clothing tightly to make them small, and putting flat and/or soft objects (such as first aid kits) against the walls of the day pack, you'll be surprised at how much you can cram into such a small space. If your pack feels "lopsided," then you have to re-pack and center the distribution of weight. Otherwise you will spend the trip and valuable energy fighting to keep your balance.

For comfort, carry heavyweight items high in the pack, otherwise, carried low, your body will have to compensate by leaning far forward, and this stresses the back. This is especially important for females as they have a naturally lower center of gravity than males. Carry or hang your cameras and camcorders around the neck or wherever they are easily accessible.

Clothing

While Mt. Whitney has been climbed in Bermuda shorts, bathing suits and leotards, correct clothing is the one item that can save your life in the event you are caught in one of the spontaneous storms that plague the Sierra Nevada. Although you are going to be hiking at the height of summer, and the temperatures down in Lone Pine will be pushing 100 degrees Fahrenheit, nearing the summit of Whitney on a totally cloudless day you can be greeted by winds of 50 MPH or more and windchill factors of freezing. Be aware that summer snowstorms and occasional Labor Day blizzards are the rule, not the exception.

Dress in layers and remove clothing as it gets warm. If it's going to be a hot day, wear the minimum if you wish, BUT *CARRY* THE MAXIMUM.

Rule Number One: Do not wear cotton clothing. Cotton kills! It absorbs enormous amounts of sweat and moisture, and is a major factor in producing hypothermia!

• Underwear — Carry with you a synthetic (again, <u>not</u> cotton) long underwear top and "long johns." You may never use them, but always have them available.

• Coats — A waterproof and windproof overcoat or parka is mandatory even though you may never use it. The best of these are the Gore-Tex® Outerwear™ line of clothing which can also supply you with the most complete and best line of "breathable" wind and water protective clothing from head to foot. To find the dealer nearest to you, call 1-800-431-GORE.

• Sweaters — A wool sweater is good to carry to wear under your water/windproof overcoat or parka. If you have problems wearing wool, fleece sweaters (also available from better outfitting chains) are excellent. Avoid ponchos as they can make you nearly "airborne" in high winds. As extra insurance, throw in a lightweight rain slicker and "space blanket" for added protection against storms.

Shoes

Many people have successfully climbed Mt Whitney in tennis shoes and sandals. This is not recommended as parts of the trail are polished granite covered by thin layers of sand. This becomes slick as glass. These types of shoes are inappropriate since the soles have very little traction. Also, they have no ankle support which you will need in some of the loose rock areas towards the summit. Almost every year a hiker will be airlifted or carried out because of ankle injuries.

Again, check at reputable sporting good chains, preferably for ankle-supported lightweight hiking shoes. Lightweight shoes save energy. A pound is a pound no matter where you wear it; any extra pound on your feet is going to tire you as if it were several pounds on your back. Since the Whitney Trail is rather easy on shoes as far as mountain trails are concerned, a quality name canvas shoe can be substituted for leather. You need not spend a fortune on shoes and you can always wait for holiday "sales" for deals on the better and more expensive brands.

You may want to try on a shoe one to one-and-a-half sizes larger than you normally wear because, in the course of the hike, your feet will swell and ideally you will be wearing 2 pairs of socks — a heavier pair over thin liners. This will cut down the chances of blisters which, needless to say, would put a quick end to any chance for the summit. Carry spare socks in case you should slip off into the water at a stream crossing. Also, if unforeseen cold winds kick up, socks double perfectly as mittens.

Hats, Eye and Sun Protection

Mandatory — The sunlight at high altitudes is pure and burns much quicker and more intensely than at sea level, even on cloudy days. For this reason, sun glasses, especially those with side protectors, are also recommended. A baseball, fishing or "Foreign Legion"-type cap is best because the rear of wide-brimmed "sombrero" straw hats tend to catch on your backpack and will literally shred to pieces in high winds. Also, take along a parka cap, wool or fleece beanie, or knit ski mask since they are light and easy to pack. Should the weather become suddenly inclement, 40% to 50% of your body heat will be lost from the head/neck area. Even if you are not fair-skinned, take along sunscreen of at least 30 SPF.

Optional — Ski goggles will protect your eyes from very severe, icy winds.

OTHER BASICS: *(See Photo #3)*

Lighting

Mandatory — You will be on the trail long before dawn and most likely be coming back down after dark. If you do not have the advantage of a full moon with you, the nights in the Sierra Nevada are sudden and absolute.

There are many types from which to choose, from hand-held flashlights and mini-lanterns to "coal miner's headlamps." Be sure to bring extra, fresh batteries and extra bulbs. Remember that although the summer days are long, after the summer solstice in June, the days will get progressively shorter. Whereas you had light until almost 9PM in early July, by early September you will have

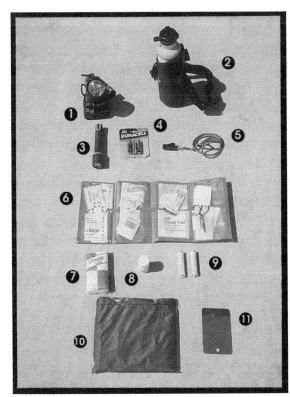

1. Headlamp
2. Extra water flask
3. Spare flashlight
4. Extra batteries
5. Emergency whistle
6. First Aid kit
7. Kleenex/tissue
8. Tylenol
9. Antacids
10. Lightweight raincoat
11. Signal mirror

Optional but important: I.D. and emergency phone numbers.

Photo #3: Basic Supplies

total darkness at the same hour. The trail is impossible to see and very dangerous in the Sierra darkness. Without lighting, your choices would be negotiating the trail by feeling for it on your hands and knees, or sitting it out until the dawn light. Not everyone in your group will require lighting equipment; usually a couple of people can follow one person with a headlamp or flashlight.

First Aid Kit

Mandatory — For illness due to altitude, abrasions and cuts due to slips and falls, and blistered feet, the following

are highly suggested contents:

> Ibuprofen
> Tylenol
> Wash-ups (available in sealed packets)
> Moleskin (for blisters)
> Kleenex packet (for nosebleeds or toilet use)
> Lip balm
> Triangle bandages with large safety pins
> Band-Aids (various sizes)
> Chewable antacids

Optional — Insect repellent; however, there's only a brief problem with mosquitoes between Lone Pine Lake and Bighorn Park/Outpost Camp, and this is usually worst in late spring to early summer.

Walking Stick

Optional — One or two can be used; recommended for the short of stature or middle-aged as they function as a 3rd or 4th leg much like "front-wheel drive" allowing the arms to relieve the legs of some of the upward burden. Also, on the return trip down, sticks can act as a brake when tired, shaky legs can buckle at the knees or one slips on the slick sand-covered rocks.

A walking stick can be a gnarled hardwood stick (very attractive ones in all sizes can be purchased at the Whitney Portal store for reasonable prices), custom walking sticks, ski poles, or simply a homemade job fashioned out of a mop handle and rubber bicycle hand grip.

Ham Radios and Cellular Phones

Definitely bring them along. Tests prove that a cellular phone call from the summit cabin will reach emergency operation headquarters in Lone Pine. Even if you do not use them for yourself, you may come across a hiker who is in an emergency situation.

Identification

If you hike alone and sickness or injury causes you to lose consciousness, no one will know who you are or whom to contact in case of emergency. Carry a current driver's license or picture I.D., and also carry notification phone numbers of relatives or friends. A handwritten and signed consent for medical treatment can also be helpful.

Cameras and Camcorders

What?
Leave them home and not document your success?
For lightweight, last minute, reliable cameras, bring some Kodak disposables (*especially* the Panorama version).
Bring extra camcorder batteries, too.

Firearms

Not allowed in Inyo or Sequoia National Parks.

Pets*

Although you'll see some being brought along for short

hikes, dogs are forbidden in Sequoia National Park. Besides, altitude is just as hard on unconditioned dogs as it is on people, and the rocky trail tears up soft dog paws. Do you want to bring along a dog that you might end up *carrying* off the mountain?

* If you bring along a dog that you must leave in your vehicle which is parked in shade, be aware that as the sun moves, so does the shade. Even though it's cool at the Whitney Portal in the morning, afternoon temperatures can heat the interior of a vehicle to well over a hundred degrees!

FOOD AND WATER

Water

Since water is one of the most crucial components of a successful trip, it is very important that you include an adequate supply for numerous reasons.

The high altitude and dryness of the Sierra Nevada causes extensive and rapid dehydration. As previously stated, with little oxygen you'll find yourself gulping air by mouth-breathing rather than breathing through your nose. This causes huge amounts of moisture to be lost from the body via the respiratory system. And, **since dehydration hastens the onset of altitude sickness**, everyone should drink more than they can reasonably carry (4-5 quarts). The best solution for this is to bring 2-3 quarts and refill them from native water sources.

Because of the extensive invasion of humanity upon Mt. Whitney, all of the pristine-appearing water sources along the trail should be regarded as undrinkable in their natural state due to the existence of the *Giardias Lamblia.* This protozoa, referred to on the trail as "Giardia" (gee-ar´dee-uh), causes severe dysentery-like symptoms.

There are ways to treat the local water for this, such as filters or iodine tablets, but they are no guarantee against waterborne bacteria and viruses carried by local wildlife. Also, iodine tablets can take up to 20 minutes to sterilize water (and still leave an iodine aftertaste), and when you're doing a round trip of Whitney in a day, each minute is at a premium. So have the iodine working on your water as you carry it in a canteen. If you desire to cut down on backpack weight by drinking the local water, there are commercial iodine taste dissolvers.

Therefore, it is wise to take your own bottled water in amounts commensurate to your weight and sex. A teenager or five-foot-tall woman will need less than a man six feet and taller. *(See Photo #4)*

The one-liter bottles of purified water sold in supermarkets are ideal as they come with a pop-up drinking spigot and lid to avoid spillage in your pack. They also withstand freezing so that you can freeze them solid prior to your journey and they will melt as your day hike progresses, ensuring that you will have tasty ice water for the entire trip. Part of the problem with dehydration is that air-temperature water is a turnoff for a lot of people, and they will be reluctant to drink enough.

Tests show that cold water empties from the stomach at a quicker rate than air-temperature water and is absorbed into the body faster. Also, because the ice cold bottles serve as a "refrigerator" for any perishable foods you bring along, the risks of botulism or salmonella-type food poisoning will be greatly lessened. Remember, 1-liter bottles weigh more than 2 pounds apiece; a few bottles add up quickly. Balance your bottles on either side of your day pack for equal weight distribution. And make them *very* accessible!

Fruit juices should not be used as part of your fluid supply. Not only does the acid content make you more susceptible to altitude sickness, juices are absorbed into the body at a slower rate. However, if you must have them, they should be diluted with water. In place of fruit juices, the best bets are the sports drinks (available in many new and improved flavors) which contain carbohydrates, glucose and sucrose for replenishment of glycogen in muscles and in replacing electrolytes. To save weight, there are electrolytes in powdered forms to add to your water. These are available at any supermarket in the powdered drink section, or sporting goods stores, or for last minute shopping, at the Whitney Portal Store. These powders will also help in disguising the iodine taste in treated local water.

WARNING — Other than a cup of coffee to start your morning, avoid drinks such as tea, colas, or any pep drugs containing caffeine as it is a diuretic and will dehydrate you even more. Get your energy boosts from sugars and candy, not stimulants. Also, AVOID salt tablets on hot days. The body will attempt to expel it via increased urination and leave you even more dehydrated. As stated in the chapter on Hazards (Dehydration), moderate salt is needed to maintain a chemical balance, but take it in lightly salted foods.

Food

To hell with the diet! Barring rich, fatty, and high protein snack foods such as cheeses, beef jerky, etc. (they also hasten the onset of altitude sickness), you are encouraged to take whatever carbohydrate foods you like in whatever quantities you can manage. Carbohydrates even help you retain water. Eating one pound of carbohydrates will cause the body to retain several pounds of water.

In some people, altitude is an appetite suppressant causing nausea and indigestion, yet it causes others to become *ravenous*. To repeat, you could lose up to six pounds or more in one day due to dehydration and caloric expenditure. This is not the time to try something new; bring only your favorite foods. If you keep on eating, you'll keep on walking!

The easiest form to carry food is in sandwiches using high-fiber, high-carbohydrate breads. Pack them in sandwich bags and then a layer of aluminum foil so that in case of a leaky water bottle they are not soaked. Use your favorite condiments to make sandwiches "juicy;" they go down a lot easier when not dry and don't use as much water to digest.

If fruit is taken, it will be bulky and a weight additive to your pack. Also, you will need a small trash bag to carry out fruit peels. **DO NOT** throw them on the trail or into bushes. Imagine the impact on the environment if every one of the thousands of hikers each year threw away the peel of but one orange or banana. Dehydrated fruit and *dry*-roasted trail mixes are good substitutes. Muffins, bagels, candy and high energy sports bars are greatly encouraged. The carbohydrates, high sugar content and palatability can be the savior of a hiker who has lost his or her appetite and is beginning to fail and "hit the wall." Hard Lifesaver-type candies are excellent as they keep the mouth moist, take your mind off physical discomforts, and deliver a constant stream of sugar to the body.

For insurance, a can of flavored milkshake-type nutritional supplements such as "Boost" can replace minerals quicker than food. Check the labels for high fat content. Be *sure* to take chewable or liquid antacids to quell sour stomach and heartburn caused by high altitude nausea.

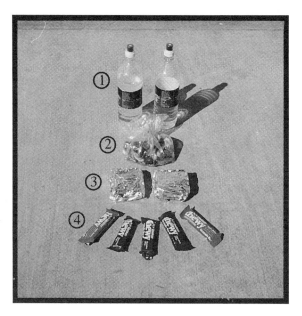

Photo #4
Minimum Food and Water Quotas
1. *One liter bottled water (taken in amounts commensurate with your weight and size*
2. *Hard candy, dried fruit, nuts, trail mix*
3. *Foil-wrapped sandwiches*
4. *Granola, power or energy bars*

CHAPTER III
HAZARDS

Unfortunately, a highly significant number of deaths have occurred on Mt. Whitney, most of them caused by weather and/or weather-related phenomena, or the failure to prepare for the unexpected. Some of these fatalities may have come about because the victims were tempted to honor difficult-to-obtain permits; or they were unfamiliar with the existence and severity of summer storms; or they simply failed to heed their instincts and posted warnings. Remember that if you become ill or injured by bad weather, falls, or complications of altitude sickness, you may have to forego any attempts for the summit until the next year. The following text describes some of the conditions you can expect to encounter.

WEATHER

Enough emphasis cannot be placed on the dangers associated with weather. To repeat: On a good day in the Sierra Nevada, more perfect weather is hard to find; on a bad day, you can die. The majority of deaths that occur on Mt. Whitney are caused by lightning and hypothermia (exposure). Do not be lulled into the belief that because it's summer you will not be threatened by cold or freezing conditions. Even though the day in the Owens Valley basin may begin clear and dry with temperatures near 100 degrees, the Sierra Nevada peaks can "create their own weather" when hot, moist air from the lowlands clashes with the cold, dry air over the range. Mt. Whitney is notorious for this. Try to pick a day when the big mountain is quiet.

If you're not sure about the weather but your instincts are warning you, **HEED THEM.** You are probably right and the mountains will always be there when the skies are clear. Before your trip, check with the Mount Whitney Ranger Station or the National Weather Service. For accurate 3- to 5-day forecasts, the NWS telephone for the Sierra Nevada area is (760) 873-3213.

Lightning

The following is from the posted sign at the Whitney Summit Trail/John Muir Trail Junction.

> ### EXTREME DANGER FROM LIGHTNING
> To avoid being struck by lightning, immediately leave the area if any of the following conditions exist:
> - **Dark clouds nearby**
> - **Thunder, hail or rain**
> - **Hissing in the air**
> - **Static electricity in the hair or fingertips**
>
> **The Whitney Shelter will not offer protection. You should leave the summit and proceed to a lower elevation.**

This is truly the most frightening element of your trip should you have the misfortune to encounter it. As previously stated, when you are at altitudes of 13,000 to 14,000 feet, you can literally be inside the storm. Lightning is not something that happens only on the higher peaks; it can occur virtually anywhere, anytime on the trail in the summer, with suddenly violent, freezing storms descending upon lower elevations as far down as Lone Pine Lake and below. At 50,000 degrees Fahrenheit, lightning boils the sap in trees. One only has to examine the burned timber from the Portal area to Mirror Lake *(See Photo #5)* to see that lightning is a threat on the entire trail. Lightning deaths have occurred most frequently *inside* the "protection" of the summit cabin. And on the stark Trail Crest, there is no shelter from lightning for several miles.

Photo #5
Burned and twisted, a dead pine tree just above the Trailhead gives silent testimony to the dangers of lightning that exist along the entire trail.

If, while you climb, little clouds begin to grow larger, thicker and darker, and you can *smell* the rain, it's time to retreat. Hail is also a warning; it is *always* accompanied by lightning. If your hair stands on end and your skin prickles, a strike is imminent within seconds. **DO NOT TAKE SHELTER UNDER BOULDERS OR CAVES.** Instead, find a large, low rock in the lowest area. If your pack does not have a metal frame, put the pack on the rock and immediately roll yourself into a ball atop it, making sure that none of your body comes into contact with the earth providing a "ground" for the lightning bolt. Do not huddle together with other members of your hiking party. If one of your party is struck by lightning, remember that sometimes it is not the strike which kills, but the shock to the heart. CPR can resuscitate a person struck by lightning. It would be wise if you and everyone in your group had CPR knowledge or training.

HYPOTHERMIA

This is the *other* most common killer in the high Sierra Nevada and is commonly called "exposure." This occurs when the internal body core temperature falls below normal. This can occur at 40 degrees Fahrenheit and can be caused by not bringing adequate warm clothing, or the most common and worst cause — getting *wet.* Once you're wet, winds only compound the low temperatures. Even if you have a warm coat along, once it gets wet and the cold winds pick up, it is no longer going to protect you. If you are caught in a freezing storm and you or your group members are shivering and unable to warm up, and lightning is no hazard, IMMEDIATELY retreat to a lower, warmer elevation.

ALTITUDE

It's not the distance or the steepness that's the problem on the Whitney trail, it's the altitude! High altitudes can cause some type of symptoms (other than high-altitude sickness) even in seasoned hikers. A phenomenon known as "oxygen dumb" occurs in professional hikers who climb the tallest summits in the world. Usually occurring at elevations of 18,000 feet and over, it can begin to occur in amateur hikers at around 12,000 feet, and most definitely begins to manifest itself at the 13,777-foot Trail Crest and beyond. Symptoms other than chronic headache and nausea are the inability to make decisions, judgments, rationalizations or just plain "think straight." If, after you make a successful summit and can't quite fully remember the last 2 miles of the journey, you probably experienced being "oxygen dumb."

Prior to your attempt at Mt. Whitney, spend as much time as possible at high altitudes.

Altitude Sickness

Altitude sickness is a fact of life in the Sierra Nevada and unless you spend a large amount of time at high altitudes, you will experience this to one degree or another. When it occurs, symptoms will come on gradually or hit you like an 18-wheeler coming around a blind corner. In the *Mount Whitney Guide for Hikers and Climbers* (Hellwig and McDonald), there is an excellent list of symptoms. But the easiest way to describe altitude sickness would be for you to remember your last really severe bout with the flu or a hangover. It's very nasty; when you get it, you'll *know* it!

Symptoms are as follows:

You become very tired, sitting down, refusing to move. You want only to lie down and go to sleep, but comfortable sleep is impossible because of physical pain. Severe mental depression and despondency may cause uncontrollable crying. You may vomit up your lunch and retch with painful dry heaves; you may refuse water. Don't do this, as water is mandatory to keep the bloodstream liquid enough to carry the limited oxygen to your starving cells.

Along with a lack of oxygen at high altitudes is the low air pressure. As high altitude causes a leakage of fluids from cerebral blood vessels, the build-up begins to press on the brain. The fluids and soft tissues of the head then expand from low air pressure, e.g., the brain in its cranium, eyeballs in their sockets. Needless to say, this causes excruciating headaches; even your teeth will hurt.

If you are severely overcome by altitude sickness, the only safe procedure is to retreat to a lower altitude as soon as possible. As you descend, all symptoms will begin to fade. To guard against altitude sickness, find a mountain in the area you live in with as high an altitude as possible and take practice hikes until your body adjusts. Or, if this is not possible, try to spend a couple of days at Whitney Portal letting your body adjust — or sleep there overnight. Check with your physician on prescription altitude pills such as Diamox. As with any medication, check with your physician in regard to possible side effects.

On the journey itself, ideally you should ascend at **NO MORE** than 1 mile per hour to give the body time to adjust to the altitude. Also, do not ascend in rapid "bursts" and then rest for more than 5 minutes. Go at the rate of the slowest member of your party. A very good rule is: TORTOISE UP, RABBIT DOWN.

Altitude sickness is not to be taken lightly. It can be fatal. In extreme cases, the lungs will fill with liquid. This is called pulmonary edema. When it occurs in the brain, it is called cerebral edema. In both cases, the victim should immediately retreat off the mountain. Warning: If you continue onward while sick, you may become so incapacitated by pain you will be unable to go up or down. The night you have to spend on the mountain without the protection of tent and/or sleeping bag will be miserable if not downright life-threatening.

If you need intense altitude exposure and you have time, another excellent hike is White Mountain Peak in the White Mountain Range (home of the ancient bristlecones). The range is an easy drive east out of Big Pine and no permits are needed. Consult your map for directions. This is the third highest mountain in California at 14,250 feet. After a 16-mile, time-consuming ride on a washboard dirt road, you will be parking your car at a trailhead of almost 12,000 feet and it is only 7 miles to the summit. For details, contact the White Mountain Ranger Station, 798 N. Main Street, Bishop, CA 93514, (760) 873-2500.

However, this extraordinarily scenic mountain range is *extremely* fragile and there are no services (food, water, gas) for miles. Use the same respect as you would for the Sierra Nevada. Also, be aware that the same dangers that exist on the Whitney Trail (sudden severe lightning storms, hypothermia, altitude) are present on the barren, tundra-covered White Mountain Trail.

DEHYDRATION

As stated in the "SUPPLIES" chapter, the most important "fuel" on this trip will be fluids — even more so than food. Due to the dry, high altitude thin air, each cell will be screaming for oxygen. Your body will be working on a frantic overtime to deliver. As you climb in the rarefied air, you will be gulping for air by mouth-breathing. Extreme amounts of water will be lost from your system via the lungs. As liquids are lost, the blood becomes thickened. Thickened blood cannot deliver its oxygenated payload into the smaller veins and capillaries of the extremities and vital organs. Those parts of the body not receiving oxygenated blood cannot continue to function efficiently. If you feel your fingers, toes and lips becoming numb, you are rapidly dehydrating and your extremities will be susceptible to the damages of cold weather. If you wait until you're really thirsty before you drink, you may hit the wall more rapidly than if you're hydrated. Make at least one water stop per half hour to replenish your lost fluids.

However, hydration can be overdone. Do not drink water to the extent you are washing out sodium (salt) and electrolytes. Fluids with electrolytes (sports drinks), saltine crackers and pretzels in moderation can help maintain an internal chemical balance. Also, do not use this trip to lose those five extra pounds that just won't come off. Give your body all the help it will need.

Tests show that even a tiny decrease in body weight due to dehydration can cut your body's physical abilities 8%-10%. This little margin of efficiency could mean making the summit, or hitting the wall and failing at the last mile! If you experience these symptoms, immediately boost your intake of fluids.

FALLS

Each year the odds are high a hiker will fall or slip, injuring an ankle or breaking a leg on ice, snow or wet rocks in creek crossings. Watch for "black ice" (an invisible, thin coating of ice) which can be presented on any part of the trail above Lone Pine Lake and especially above Trail Camp—sometimes all season long.

BEARS

Since the late 90's, the bear problem has escalated dramatically. The stealing of food by American black bears has now extended from the Portal to Lone Pine Lake, Outpost Camp, and all the way up to Trail Camp. Damage to cars at the Portal has also increased. Bears have an incredible sense of smell. To avoid a smashed window or peeled-off door (yes, they're that strong), strip your vehicles and trunks of all food wrappers, chewing gum, chap stick, soap, toothpaste, human and vehicle deodorants, bug sprays (all these products smell like fruit to bears), and old food under the seats. Also conceal or take ice chests out of cars. Bears know the shape of a covered ice chest.

Bear canisters (bear-proof containers to store food) are now required and mandatory for overnight hikers up to Trail Camp. Canisters can be rented at the Mount Whitney Ranger Station, any sporting goods store in Lone Pine, and the Portal store. There are no trees above Mirror Lake to hang food, and bears have figured out how to retrieve food hung over boulders.

Backpacks left outside with food are being dragged away or destroyed by bears right there at Trail Camp, and you will risk a great threat of injury if you place food inside your tent with you.

To put it simply: If you don't have anything to eat for breakfast, getting to the summit will be all that much more difficult.

THESE RULES DO NOT APPLY TO DAY HIKERS!

Hikers may see or hear bears at Whitney Portal and on any part of the trail (except beyond Trail Camp) in the predawn hours, but so far, the bears are avoiding close human contact.

Because this is a long trip with its dangers, it is wise to take along a hiking partner or else carry along ham radios (FCC license required) or cellular phones for contact with emergency services. But because batteries can fail, if you hike alone, back yourself up with a phone call to relatives when you return. There are no phones at Whitney Portal or the Whitney Portal store, so you'll have to allot a half hour to return to Lone Pine to alert relatives or friends that you are down safely. It's also a good idea to leave the phone number of the Inyo County Sheriff/Search & Rescue in case you are injured so that a search party can be sent out if necessary. The phone number for the Sheriff's Office in Lone Pine is (619) 876-5606.

CHAPTER IV
TRAIL NOTES
Some Last Tips

Hopefully, these following tips taken from personal triumphs and failures can assist you on your journey:

1. Breakfast — Even though there is an all-night cafe in Lone Pine, starting your hike with a huge, fat-laden breakfast may be more of a hindrance than help. You will be on the trail mere minutes after you eat, and your body's precious energy and blood supply will be diverted towards digestion. This will cause you to be so lethargic, you might drop out after a couple of miles. The last heavy meal should be lunch the day before so that it has time to get into your fat reserves. The night before your journey, enjoy a normal dinner, but go light with a sweet role and coffee on the morning of the big day. If you simply cannot function without a hot, classic breakfast, order small portions.

2. Perspective — Do not think of the journey in its entirety of 10.7 miles. The sheer magnitude of the ordeal on which you are about to embark will intimidate and overwhelm you. Visualize the trip in mile/hour increments (e.g., "In two-and-a-half hours I'll be at Lone Pine Lake; 35 minutes after that I'll be at Bighorn Park; lunch time will be at Trail Crest," etc.).

3. Confusion — If you get lost due to snow on the trail, follow the notches on the trees. Above the last tree at 4.9 miles, there are no trail markers. If you do find yourself lost, **STOP** and **WAIT** for other hikers to come along. During daylight hours, there are *always* more hikers on the trail. Do not waste valuable energy trampling the

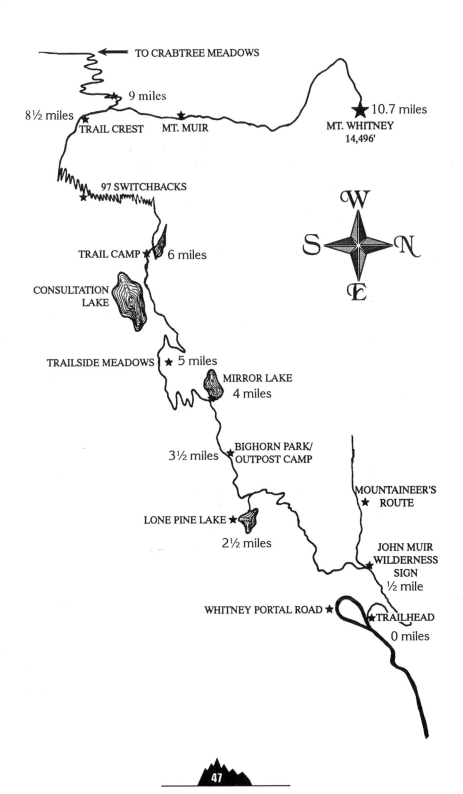

TO CRABTREE MEADOWS

9 miles

8½ miles
TRAIL CREST   MT. MUIR

10.7 miles
MT. WHITNEY
14,496'

W
S ✦ N
E

97 SWITCHBACKS

TRAIL CAMP ★ 6 miles

CONSULTATION
LAKE

TRAILSIDE MEADOWS ★ 5 miles

MIRROR LAKE
4 miles

3½ miles ★ BIGHORN PARK/
OUTPOST CAMP

MOUNTAINEER'S
★ ROUTE

LONE PINE LAKE ★

2½ miles

JOHN MUIR
WILDERNESS
SIGN
½ mile

WHITNEY PORTAL ROAD ★   ★ TRAILHEAD

0 miles

fragile ecology by walking around in circles for twenty minutes.

4. Very Important — Don't think that because you're not young, you will fail. Often a strong will, developed as we mature and experience numerous defeats, gives us the determination to triumph over those who are younger and more fit.

And last, but not least:

The "3 Rs"

Rules —
> READ and HEED all posted U.S. Forestry regulations.

Reason —
> This is a big, dangerous mountain.
> **USE COMMON SENSE.** In the case of weather, listen to and trust your instincts. If you become ill or injured by altitude or weather, immediately retreat off the mountain.

Respect —
> Don't "blow" slower hikers off the trail. Announce that you're coming through. Whenever possible, relinquish the trail to those coming up and/or are heavily loaded. It's much easier to regain momentum if you're going down as opposed to up.
>
> Pack out all trash: gum, gum wrappers, cigarette packages and butts, fruit peels and

food wrappings. Leave the mountain as if you'd never been there. Bury all human waste 6 inches deep and at least 100 feet away from water sources. If you find the litter of a careless hiker, pack it out.

FINALLY. . .

DON'T CUT SWITCHBACKS!
This will cause erosion on the already overtaxed Whitney trail. It only takes a few seconds and feet to follow the designated trail.

CHAPTER V
THE ASCENT

The following time measurements are an *average* only.
It will not be possible to adhere to these exact times if
numerous rest stops or video and photo opportunities are
made. The better your condition, the less rest stops you'll
need. A comfortable speed is one mile per hour. Those in
better condition and acclimatization can approximate their
summit arrival with 45- to 50-minute miles. If you have to
stop briefly every 100 steps or so to catch your breath,
that's normal and may assist you to a successful summit.

The starting hour of 4:00 A.M. is a suggestion only. Some
may wish to start at an earlier or later hour. Average starts
are 4:00, 5:00 and 6:00 A.M.

Moonlight Ascents —

The following time measurements can be used for these
ascents, but be advised that, if you start before midnight,
you are technically on the mountain for <u>two</u> dates (2
days) and will therefore need an overnight permit. Thus,
starting after midnight will eradicate this problem. Consult
a calendar as to when the full moon will be rising and
crossing over the trail with you. However, take some kind
of lighting; below the timberline, the dense forests are
dark and the rising moon will go behind Candlelight Peak
(the mountain south of Whitney Portal/Trailhead) for
some time. Plus, the Sierra Nevada nights, even at the
height of summer, can be *very* cold and often windy. Take
clothing that will keep you warm and safe.

"Trail Condition" will describe cleanliness, clarity and

steepness of each portion of the trail combined with the ease to climb it.

"Trail Speed" denotes how fast you will be able to negotiate a certain portion of the trail when altitude, exhaustion, distance and hours affect your performance.

TIME CHART

The following times are taken from each posted location sign to the next:

ASCENT — *(Approximately 10 hours, 20 minutes)*

Trail Head to John Muir Wilderness/ Mountaineer's Route..........................	30 minutes
Wilderness/Mountaineer's Route sign to Lone Pine Lake...................................	2 hours
Lone Pine Lake to Bighorn Park/ Outpost Camp*...........................	35-40 minutes
Bighorn Park/Outpost Camp to Mirror Lake......................................	25 minutes
Mirror Lake to Trailside Meadows..................	1 hour
Trailside Meadows to Trail Camp...................	1 hour
Trail Camp to Trail Crest...........................	2½ hours
Trail Crest to Summit.................................	2 hours

* (Being in the same area and only 5 minutes apart from sign to sign, this location counts as one.)

Photo #6
Adventure begins with the first step.

Trailhead: Altitude: 8,361 feet

Hour: 4:00 A.M.
Mile: 0
Trail Condition: Sandy, good
Trail Speed: Fast

It's 4:00 A.M. You are standing in the darkness at the Whitney Portal Trailhead. You are packed with everything you'll need for the trip, including emergency situations. You have acclimated and conditioned your body. You are going to adhere to U.S. Forestry rules and regulations. **You are familiar with the dangers associated with this trip.** You are going to use common sense.

Fine! You are now on your way. Remember: TORTOISE UP, RABBIT DOWN.

From here to Lone Pine Lake is one of the toughest parts of the journey in that, although the trail is clearly marked sand and decomposed granite with a few rocky sections, it's moderately steep. Added to the hour being predawn, your metabolism may be sluggish and your body cold and hard to start. Lighting is mandatory. Depending on the month, you will not get adequate sunlight until almost 6:00 A.M.

John Muir Wilderness sign (fork)

Hour: 4:30 a.m.
Mile: ½
Trail Condition: Sandy, well marked, somewhat steep
Trail Speed: Fast

*Photo #7: John Muir Wilderness/Mountaineer's Route sign
The well-marked Whitney Trail is straight ahead.*

A large U.S. Forestry billboard is posted here with tips for succeeding, plus weekly updates on existing conditions of the trail up ahead. *(See Photo #7.)* Stay on the main trail. To the right (northwest) the fork leads up steeply to the difficult "Mountaineer's Route. The main trail will be wide and clearly marked with some cutaways through rocky areas. Past the fork, the trail starts with ten long switch-backs, then straightens and climbs steeply for less than ¼ mile. Rest frequently at this point, but don't quit. Immediately you begin about 18 difficult switchbacks through the pines which change to a treeless, chaparral-covered stretch, then the trail once again levels as you approach:

Lone Pine Lake: Altitude: 9,960 feet

Hour: 6:30 A.M.
Mile: 2.5
Trail Condition: Sandy, clearly marked
Trail Speed: Fast

Photo #8
Lone Pine Lake as seen from the Whitney Trail.

An extraordinarily scenic little lake perched on the lip of a rock cliff is off a few hundred feet to your left (southeast). Here, you should be catching your second wind and your body will be sufficiently warmed up. Stay on the trail, bear to the right (southwest), and catch the trail through a dry stream bed into a sandy glacial scoop.

Follow the trail to the left of the broken tree trunk *(See Photo #9)*, then bear to the right (north) towards the rocky southern cliffs of Mt. Thor.

Early in the season, if snow is present on the trail, follow the carved notches on the trees.

Photo #9
Just out of Lone Pine Lake, pick up the
trail to the left of the dead tree,
then bear to the right (north).

Begin up 17 easy switchbacks along the southern cliffs of Mt. Thor. At switchback #8 there is a faded "3-mile" marker on a rock 20 minutes out of Lone Pine Lake (6:50 A.M.) *(See Photo #10.)*

Photo #10
The 3-mile point on the southern flank of Mt. Thor,
half way between Lone Pine Lake and Bighorn Park/Outpost Camp.

Bighorn Park/Outpost Camp: Altitude: 10,365 feet

Hour: 7:10 A.M.
Mile: 3.5 and 3.8, respectively
Trail Condition: Sandy, well-marked, gentle grade
Trail Speed: Very fast

Once you have arrived at the posted sign on the overlook of Bighorn Park, the Whitney crest will come into view. The points of Trail Crest topping the 97 switchbacks can be seen off to the west along with the upper portion of the switchbacks. With sharp eyes, you can see hikers on the 97 switchbacks approaching Trail Crest. Also, the Whitney massif near the Third Needle section will be visible. *(See Photo #11.)* At last, you'll feel you're making some progress. Descend into Bighorn Park 100 yards via the three switchbacks and into the large, marshy meadow. This will be the last relief from the relentless ascencion (5 miles) until Trail Crest. Take into account you will have to walk *up* this path on your return journey and will have to reserve energy for it.

Photo #11
After hours of being hidden by forest, your objective, the Mount Whitney crest (in the background) finally comes into view, giving you a welcomed sense of confidence to go on.

Catch the two log bridges over the streams, bearing left (south) all the way. Follow the trail as it skirts along the base of a large rock cliff. Have your camera ready. The rising midsummer sun will promise you a gallery of spectacular photos as the granite slopes of Mt. Thor turn from blazing coral to brilliant gold.

In 5 minutes, as you walk in the direction of a photogenic, roaring waterfall, you will be in Outpost Camp. This will be your first chance to use the solar toilets (open only on weekends).

Follow the sign north (to your right) to the solar toilet. The trail forks here and will be clearly marked. Pick up the trail again to the left (southwest) up a series of switchbacks, across the southern escarpment of Mount Thor, and the eastern glacial shelf of Mirror Lake. A man-made rock "staircase" (under water in heavy snow thaws) leads you up the approach to. . .

Photo #12
Looking down upon Mirror Lake after passing out of the timberline.

Mirror Lake: Altitude: 10,640 feet *(See Photo #12)*

Hour: 7:35 A.M.
Mile: 4.0
Trail Condition: Steeply inclines; cutaways through
        boulder fields; tall steps in places
Trail Speed: Moderate

Before you get close to the eastern shores of this pictur-
esque lake, the trail will bear left (south) and begin winding up a huge granite escarpment. The going becomes a
little difficult for older or short people. The trail changes
from mostly sand to steps cut away through solid granite
much like a staircase with steps more than a foot high in
some places. From here to Trailside Meadows, trees
immediately become scarcer until you finally climb out of
the timberline. At any point on this portion of the trail, the
views in all directions are *spectacular! (See Photo #13.)*

Photo #13
Nearing Trailside Meadows, you're up high enough to see (1) Mirror
Lake , (2) Bighorn Park/Outpost Camp and (3) Lone Pine Lake .

Photo #14: Trailside Meadows
At approximately 5 miles and slightly less than half way to the
summit, Trailside Meadows is a good spot for lunch
to replenish your energy stores.

Trailside Meadows: Altitude: 11,359 feet *(See Photo #14)*

Hour: 8:35 A.M.
Mile: 5.0
Trail Condition: Granite cutaways, soft and sandy;
   slippery in places
Trail Speed: Fast

You're roughly half way to the summit!

This beautiful, lush little meadow, with its rushing stream
against a thundering waterfall, is a great place for lunch
(along with Consultation Lake just up the trail at 9:15
A.M.); further on, the altitude may begin to affect your
appetite. Bear up and to the right as the trail begins to

climb sharply and eastward for a few moderate switchbacks, then back west again. *(5 mi. marker on rock.)*

About half an hour out, Consultation Lake will be visible
on your left (south). As you come up the winding trail of a
pinnacle-like rock overlooking Consultation Lake, signs
giving you directions to the solar toilet will give you hope
that you have finally reached the easternmost stretches of
Trail Camp.

Photo #15: Trail Camp
If altitude is going to affect you, it will begin to manifest itself here.
This is the last private solar toilet available and another good place
to eat or rest before taking on the dreaded switchbacks just ahead.

Trail Camp: Altitude: 12,039 feet

Hour: 9:35 a.m.
Mile: 6.3

Trail Condition: Granite cutaways and soft sand; slippery
    in places
Trail Speed: Fast

This is the camping area for the lucky ones with overnight
permits. The last water on the trail will be here, but it is to
be considered unsuitable for drinking without Giardia
treatment. Also, this will be your last chance to use a
solar toilet (other than the modest open-air "outhouse"
on the summit) and there will be little privacy for these
matters later up the mountain. If altitude is beginning to
affect your performance, eat lunch here and keep your
"engine" fueled. And if altitude sickness *is* to occur it will
most likely begin to manifest itself at this location. It is not
uncommon to see your fellow day hikers (the ones who
did not heed the "tortoise up" warning) lying prone with
severe headaches, nausea and vomiting.

Photo #16: Mount Whitney From Trail Camp
The Whitney Crest from Trail Camp — from left: (1)-Third; (2)-Crooks
Peak (formerly Day Needle); (3)-Keeler Needle; 4-Whitney Summit.
So close and yet so far!

Should you decide to leave your backpack containing food at Trail Camp (not recommended), be aware that marmots (large woodchuck-like rodents) have become as bold as the bears and will pilfer and/or chew an unattended backpack in broad daylight. Take all valuables with you.

(Enjoy a 15-minute rest/lunch stop at this point.)

97* Switchbacks: Altitude: 12,039+ feet
Also known as 96 or 97. Opinions on exact count differ. Only feels like more when you're climbing them.)

Hour: 9:50 A.M.
Mile: 6.3
Trail Condition: Steep! Loose talus rock; seepage at
        bottom; clearly marked sand and rock near
        summit
Trail Speed: Moderate speed at base; fast near summit

Immediately out of Trail Camp, you will begin what is regarded by most as the most difficult part of the journey. It is tedious, monotonous, and steep — a trail in which you cannot see yourself gaining any progress until the last ½ mile and with an altitude gain of 1,738 feet in 2½ miles.

These are the legendary, infamous, and reviled *switchbacks* which, coupled with the steepness and altitude gain, weeds out the winners from the losers. How you approach the switchbacks, both mentally and physically, can be the deciding point between victory and failure for the day.

Break out your favorite candy bars; you're going to need them from here to Trail Crest. The secret of success here will be a slow, steady pace — baby steps, if you will. The temptation to quit will be great, but remember: **This part of the journey is only 2½ hours out of your *entire life*,** and the reward of what lies ahead is worth the misery. Except for the altitude gain and 6 hours of hiking behind you, the trail begins fairly easy by traversing the moraine directly west out of Trail Camp. *(See Photo #17.)* This part of the trail rates as a moderate pace due to the trail being comprised of loose rock wetted by the seepage of melting snow.

Photo #17:
Switchbacks
From
Trail Camp

From Trail Camp, hikers begin the toughest challenge of the Whitney trail, the 97 switchbacks. The trail begins by traversing the moraine (center right) and then zig-zagging all the way to Trail Crest (see arrow). To give an idea of scale, on the day this photo was taken, there were a hundred hikers visible in the background, but distance turns them into mere specks.

At close to the half-way point *(See Photo #18)*, you will cross a slick, gray section of granite. Cable hand-rails have been installed for safety on this part of the trail because of ice and melting snowfields early in the season, sometimes year around.

Photo #18
Black ice, melting-snow well into the season, and a long slide down into the "bowl" necessitate cable hand-rails approaching the half-way point on the 97 switchbacks.

From these cables is where your mental fortitude and determination must come into play to put you "over the top." Here is where the topography changes so that the slope of the mountain will allow you to see many of the switchbacks above you for hundreds of feet. Try not to look up. Seeing other hikers zig-zagging zombie-like several stories above you makes the climb seem endless. This is where many hikers give up, give in, and drop out. *(See Photo #19.)*

Photo #19
An aerial view of the 97
switchbacks up to Trail Crest (arrow)

Photo #20
At the 8-mile point on the 97 switchbacks, altitude and distance begin to take their toll on a tired hiker $1/_5$ mile from Trail Crest.

Approaching the 8-mile point might still be a fading 8-mile marker on a rock. *(See Photo #20.)* Once you have made it here, it is but $1/_5$ of a mile to Trail Crest. When you get high enough to the "points" of Trail Crest, the breathtaking vista to the west — which is King's Canyon and Sequoia National Park — will come into view. Just seeing this indescribable panorama will erase the trauma of the last 2½ hours, and a mental second wind or "rush" will take you to. . .

Trail Crest: Altitude: 13,777 feet *(See Photos #21 & #22)*

Hour: 12:20 P.M.
Miles: 8.5
Trail Condition: Loose rock; narrow and winding
Trail Speed: Slow

Photo #21
Some of the rock formations at the entrance to Sequoia National Park
(at Trail Crest)

Great! The most boring segment of the journey is over
and you are to be commended. If you thought the eastern
face of the Sierra Nevada was something, you've got to
see the western valley that's been hidden. Drink in a view

that will take your breath away! Strangers will congratulate you with a "high five," and your thrill at having defeated the 97 switchbacks will re-fortify you enough to proceed to the summit. If you are hungry, this is a great place — along with other hikers who made it — to replenish your store of energy. Have a snack or lunch while you savor the Big Sky horizons of the Great Western Divide that cannot quite be captured in words, photos or videos; it *must* be experienced in person.

Photo #22: View Of Sequoia National Park
Just down from Trail Crest, the views into Sequoia National Park
and the Great Western Divide are phenomenal!
But be careful; it's hundreds of feet down into the valley.
That's Hitchcock Lake at center left.

Now it's time to take on the last two and *toughest* miles of the journey (other than the 2nd mile of the return trip). Even though once you've crossed over the backside of the crest, you are not ascending at nearly the steepness of the first 8½ miles, late hour of day, altitude, distance and physical stress will begin to take their toll.

Follow the trail to your right and begin skirting the rock ledges. Initially, the trail will drop a gradual 300 feet in elevation for the first ½ mile (much to your relief), but keep in mind that you must make up this drop on your return from the summit and you will be extremely tired. Reserve energy for this section.

Whitney Summit Trail/John Muir Trail Junction:
Altitude: 13,480 feet

Hour: 12:35 P.M.
Mile: 9.0
Trail Condition: Narrow, winding; loose rock; brief
        boulder climbing; poorly delineated after
        some hard winter seasons
Trail Speed: Very slow and cautious

Make sure you stay on the Whitney Trail (to the north) and do not begin wrongly descending the John Muir Trail (west) down into Crabtree Meadows. It will take precious time and energy to climb up out of there. If in doubt, wait until a seasoned hiker comes by, and don't be embarrassed to ask for directions. Hikers on the Whitney trail are the friendliest you'll find anywhere.

From here, parts of the trail are little more than a "mountain goat trail" in places as it skirts rugged and eroded rock cliffs. The topography is reminscent of the Moab valleys of Utah. In some areas, you will feel like you're crawling along the ledges of a tall skyscraper. Those with aversions to extreme height must be forewarned that in some areas, the trail drops off sharply downwards for hundreds of feet. *(See Photo #23.)*

Photo #23: Whitney Trail Facing South To Trail Crest
An example of the extreme slope of the west side of the mountain
and the loose talus-strewn trail
which makes the going slow and difficult.

This is also one of the most dangerous spots on the climb because you will be fully exposed to every kind of weather element. If a sudden thunderstorm should blow in, there is nowhere to hide and very little time in a long distance to escape. You will see the foreboding sign warning of lightning *(See Page 37 in Chapter III: Hazards)* on a turnout at the Whitney Summit Trail/John Muir Trail Junction

<u>HEED THIS SIGN!</u>

A little way from the Junction is another of the few wide turnouts where many people drop their packs. This is not recommended as you will need water (and warm clothing in the event you're caught in a freezing summer storm). Drop your pack *only* if skies are clear with absolutely no chance of a storm. If you only want to carry water, take along a lumbar or accessory pouch with holsters that carry your water flasks.

The trail from here for the next mile or so, while almost horizontal and gradual in gaining 1,016 feet to the summit, will be difficult in that it is rocky, loose, narrow and, in some places, very hard to see. There will be areas where you must climb over moderately-sized boulders, and if there are strong winds, you will just be trying to stay on the mountain. All of this just as your body begins to react to altitude, distance and physical exhaustion. Each step will be an effort. Your fellow hikers will be as tired as you and may appear catatonic or "oxygen dumb" as they walk with you.

Somewhere between the Junction and the Third Needle (the "halfway" point on Trail Crest, *See Photo #24*), you may hit the wall for the first time. *(See Map #1.)* The Mt. Whitney summit and the needles will be visible and this is the place where most people give up, their tired brains rationalizing that "This is close enough." This is the point where your mental strength must override physical limitations. From this point, it's MIND OVER MATTER! Ration each step and bit of energy and continue on.

Coming up on the Third Needle, the trail will flatten out and be easier to find. Just keep walking. Passing by Keeler Needle and Crooks Peak, reward yourself with the spectacular view between the "Windows" (the **"V"** base where the needles come together) and down into the

TRAIL CREST

MT. WHITNEY
SUMMIT

Map #1: Approximately 1 mile from Trail Crest and coming up on the Third Needle,
the first experience with "Hitting the Wall" usually occurs mentally when the summit
is in sight, and physically when the body nears the 14,000-foot altitude.

Owens Valley. There is also a window at the Third Needle with an extremely narrow footpath across it. If severe winds are present, wait between gusts to cross the windows. It's STRAIGHT DOWN for 2,000 feet!

*Photo #24: Approximately 1 mile from the summit (see arrow)
on the Whitney Trail
With the Whitney summit and cabin in view, this is where many
"hit the wall" for the first time and give up, with the rationalization
that "This is close enough."*

A little way north of Keeler Needle you will find a fading 10-mile marker on a boulder just south of an uprighted rock. *(See Photo #25.)* Beyond this point, the trail deviates into many different ones taken by thousands of hikers over the decades. Just pick the easiest route for yourself to. . .

Photo #25: Northbound At The 10-Mile Point
The Whitney summit is beyond and out of view to the top right.
Don't quit now, you're almost there!

Mt. Whitney Summit: Altitude: 14,496 feet
(See Photos #26 & #27)

Hour: 2:20 P.M.
Mile: 10.7

Incredible! You're actually there! And you *never* thought you'd make it!

Photo #26: At The Top Of The Lower 48 States Gazing Across The U.S. An aerial view of (1) Whitney Summit (with cabin); (2) Keeler Needle; (3) Crooks Peak; and (4) Third Needle as seen from the northwest.

You will be very tired and affected by altitude, but stay conscious of your surroundings. Just take in the indescribable view, such as a sky so blue it hurts, a sun white as ice, and the total silence and isolation which is at once frightening and fascinating.

Here, there will be no living things such as wildlife and fauna; on a windless day no sounds are heard except for a high flying jet or the hum of a sailplane as it rides the thermals across the east ridge. If it's a weekday and you're lucky, you might be rewarded by a military jet doing a "barrel roll" right over your head as it buzzes victorious hikers on the summit. Hikers who were strangers will shake your hand and congratulate you as a new member of the special club who has done the "Big One."

Photo #27: Aerial View Of Summit Cabin
This photo was taken on a calm and clear week in late November
when there were 3 hikers at the cabin —

As tired as you'll be, take lots of photos and videos, then go to the Summit cabin *(See Photo #28)* and the sign-in book placed outside it. You will be very tired and light-headed. It will feel good to sit down on the highest point in the contiguous United States and just take it all in.

Photo #28: Mt. Whitney Summit And Cabin
Even though the temperature was over 100° F in Lone Pine,
at the summit wind-chill factors caused just above-freezing
conditions on this cloudless, early September afternoon.

If there are cold winds, you can warm up in the comfort of the summit cabin, just don't get *too* comfortable. If you sit too long, your joints and muscles may begin to stiffen. Remember: you must get yourself down the mountain, and that unless you are in a life-threatening situation, neither Lone Pine Airport nor Search & Rescue will send a helicopter to ferry you out no matter how much you beg or offer to pay. There is no way off of Mt. Whitney but under your *own* power.*

*(To add a special extra to having made the summit, rent a plane ride from Lone Pine Airport and fly over the entire Whitney Trail. You won't believe the magnitude of your accomplishment — that you actually walked so far and so high. Of course, document your flyover in photographs and video!)

CHAPTER VI
THE DESCENT

Return Time: 6 hours 40 minutes

TIME CHART

Some descent times indicated are slow due to difficult footing on portions of the trail.

DESCENT — *(6 hours, 40 minutes)*

Summit to Trail Crest................................ 1½ hours

Trail Crest to Trail Camp........................ 1-1½ hours

Trail Camp to Trailside Meadows........... 40 minutes

Trailside Meadows to Mirror Lake........... 40 minutes

Mirror Lake to Outpost Camp/
    Bighorn Park................................ 15-20 minutes

Bighorn Park to Lone Pine Lake............. 20 minutes

Lone Pine Lake to John Muir
    Wilderness sign... 1 hour

John Muir Wilderness sign
    to Trailhead................................ 20-25 minutes

---

Summit to John Muir Trail Junction:
Altitude:14,496 feet to 13,480 feet

Departure Hour: 3:00 P.M.
Duration: 3:00 P.M. to 4:30 P.M.
Trail Speed: Fast to slow, and extremely difficult
Distance: 10.7 miles to Trailhead

The first mile back to Trail Crest will be fairly easy; it's the second mile *(See Map #2)* that will be the true test of the day.

Although it seems easy going downhill to the John Muir Trail Junction, your having just spent quite a few hours hovering slightly above and below 14,000 feet will cause physical factors that will make the going difficult.

First: There will be simple exhaustion. Move slowly and surely.

Second: A day of extreme physical exertion can cause diarrhea and vomiting. If you are experiencing altitude sickness, descending will ease your symptoms. Chewable antacids can help ease your nausea.

Whitney Trail/John Muir Trail Junction:
Altitude: 13,480 feet

Distance: 9.0 miles to Trailhead

At approximately the John Muir Trail cutoff, and the ascent to Trail Crest *(See Map #2)*, you could experience hitting the wall for the second time. You might vomit or be racked with dry heaves. Don't fight it. Just go along

TRAIL CREST

MT. WHITNEY SUMMIT

Map #2: Having spent several hours around the 13,000- to 14,000-plus-foot altitude can cause the second experience with "Hitting the Wall."

with your body's reactions to altitude and fatigue. Actually, you will feel better afterward.

Once you have regained the 300-foot climb back up towards the Junction and begin the journey down the 97 switchbacks, most of your physical ailments will be alleviated with each 1,000-foot decrease in altitude (although headaches tend to linger until last).

Trail Crest to Trail Camp:
 Altitude: 13,777 feet to 12,039 feet

Duration: 4:30 P.M. to 6:00 P.M.
Trail Speed: Ballistic!
Distance: 8.5 miles to Trailhead

Although the switchbacks were extremely miserable to ascend, coming down they are actually *fun!* Simply put one foot in front of the other. In fact, *jog* if you feel like it. As you descend, you will start restoring some of your energy lost in achieving the summit. Use the angle of the grade to make as much time as possible. With a normal walking pace, you should arrive at the cable hand-rails about 50 minutes down from Trail Crest.

Trail Camp to Trailside Meadows:
 Altitude: 12,039 feet to 11,395 feet

Duration: 6:00 P.M. to 6:30 P.M.
Trail Speed: Fast but cautious; sand on trail
Distance: 6.0 miles to Trailhead

Do not stop at Trail Camp if you don't need to use the toilet, but keep on walking. It will be late in the day and once the sun sets behind the crest, it will become cool to cold, thus stiffening muscles and causing you to tire even more.

Trailside Meadows to Mirror Lake:
Altitude: 11,395 feet to 10,640 feet

Duration: 6:30 P.M. to 7:10 P.M.
Trail Speed: Fast but cautious
Distance: 5.0 miles to Trailhead

When you ascended the trail, these were the tall rock "steps" which you struggled up. The descent time is the same as ascending due to the fact that from here down to Mirror Lake, the trail is dusted with sand, is quite slippery, and has enough of a grade to be a little hazardous. Use caution going down as you will be moving fast and anxiously to get as far down the mountain as possible before total darkness. Your walking stick will be useful here because tired legs are prone to buckling.

Mirror Lake to Outpost Camp/Bighorn Park:
Altitude: 10,640 feet to 10,365 feet

Duration: 7:10 P.M. to 7:25/7:30 P.M.
Trail Speed: Very fast
Distance: 4.0 miles to Trailhead

Do not stop at Mirror Lake unless you *must* rest. Either here or Outpost Camp is where the third incident of hitting the wall could occur.

Outpost Camp/Bighorn Park to Lone Pine Lake:
Altitude: 10,365 feet to 9,960 feet

Duration: 7:40 P.M. to 8:00 P.M. (10-minute rest period)
Trail Speed: Fast, excepting impending darkness
Distance: 3.8 miles to Trailhead

At Outpost Camp, *complete* exhaustion sets in. Physical and mental stores nearly depleted, you will be "running on empty," questioning your sanity, and tempers will be ragged and raw. This is a good place to sit down for a little while and grab a snack. But keep in mind that as you enviously watch those hikers with permits bedding down for the night, it will be very difficult to get yourself up to complete the last 3.8 miles. Some hikers will hit the wall for the third time. *(See Map #3.)* The sun will be low and you will be lonely and alone because other hikers will have gone off the trail or bedded down. Your muscles will be stiffening with cold and overuse. Summoning anything out of your energy reserves will be akin to starting a car with a weak battery.

You will need to climb the 100 yards out of Outpost Camp/ Bighorn Park with what little energy you have left. At this point of the journey, you may be exhausted to the point of tears, wondering how you will find the energy to make it back to the Portal. Fantasies of favorite creature comforts ("real" food, a cup of hot coffee, an ice-cold beer, taking off your shoes and pack, or just sitting down) may be the only incentive to keep going. But it's only a matter of minutes to Lone Pine Lake.

Map #3: With approximately 17.6 miles of hard hiking behind you, complete exhaustion sets in at Bighorn Park/Outpost Camp.

Lone Pine Lake to Trailhead:
Altitude: 9,960 feet to 8,361 feet

Duration: 8:00 P.M. to 9:20 P.M.
Trail Speed: Fast, except for darkness
Distance: 2.5 miles to Trailhead

A slight incline near the crest of the lake and then it's all blessedly downhill. Even at the height of summer, darkness will be descending at the same time you will have crossed over to the dark, east face of Mt. Thor and the sun will have set on the Sierra Crest. Here is where your flashlights are mandatory, for if the full moon is not rising as you descend, darkness will be total and it will be impossible to follow the trail. You will probably be alone on the trail and be very tired, your legs like lead. But rejoice in the fact that from here, depending on how fast you travel, the comfort of your automobile is but *ONE HOUR* and some change away.

At 9:00 P.M. you should reach the John Muir Wilderness sign/Mountaineer's Route cutoff. It's now only 20 minutes until you can finally *STOP!*

Whitney Portal

Hour: 9:20 P.M.

Major congratulations!

You're back at your car wondering what*ever* possessed you to go up in the first place or how you made it all the way back down! Be proud. Feel and savor your proud exhaustion. You've earned it, so wear it as a badge of your remarkable achievement!

EPILOGUE

As you leave the Sierra Nevada and drive down the dark mountain road, you may vow *never* again to climb Mount Whitney; you may even despise this mountain and curse its name. But as you drive into Lone Pine to bed down, or turn for home on Highway 395, the awesome reality of what you just accomplished will kick in. You'll smile to yourself and you'll begin to bask in that wonderful after-glow that only comes with success.

But when next you drive past Mount Whitney, and you tell everyone you were *up there*, you just might start planning your next trip to the top!

ABOUT THE AUTHOR

Sharon Baker-Salony is a freelance writer from Southern California. She hikes the Sierra Nevada peaks in her spare time and completed her first successful summit at 49 years of age. She's made many hikes in the Sierra Nevada and surrounding mountain ranges, and tries to make one or more one-day trips up Mount Whitney every year.

Sharon Baker-Salony